Investigating the Human Body

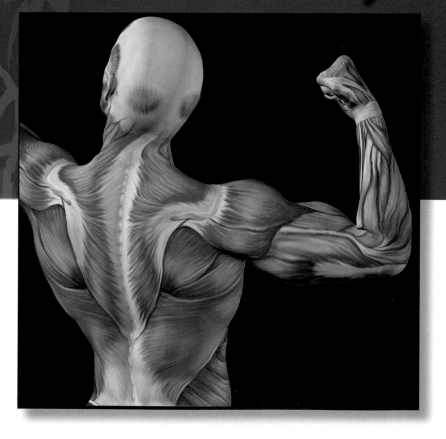

Connie Jankowski

Life Science Readers:
Investigating
the Human Body

Publishing Credits

Editorial Director
Dona Herweck Rice

Associate Editor
Joshua BishopRoby

Editor-in-Chief
Sharon Coan, M.S.Ed.

Creative Director
Lee Aucoin

Illustration Manager
Timothy J. Bradley

Publisher
Rachelle Cracchiolo, M.S.Ed.

Science Contributor
Sally Ride Science™

Science Consultants
Thomas R. Ciccone, B.S., M.A.Ed.,
   Chino Hills High School
Dr. Ronald Edwards,
   DePaul University

Teacher Created Materials
5301 Oceanus Drive
Huntington Beach, CA 92649
http://www.tcmpub.com
ISBN 978-0-7439-0595-4
© 2008 Teacher Created Materials, Inc.
Reprinted 2011
Printed in China

Table of Contents

Being Human

More that six billion humans live on earth. They look different. They act differently. They think different thoughts. However, they all share the same basic structure. Their bodies all have the same kinds of **systems** inside. This is because they are all human.

All living things have **genes**. Humans all have human genes. Genes help determine how a person will look and behave. Many things are inherited. Body size, eye color, and hair texture are all inherited. So are chances for developing certain diseases, and even personality traits. Everyone inherits the body's most important systems.

Every cell in your body has a copy of your DNA. Your DNA is a recipe for growing your whole body.

Care and Feeding of the Human Body

The human body is an amazing machine. When something in the body is not working right, there is trouble. The body cannot perform at its best. Caring for our bodies is important. First we need to understand how the body works. People with knowledge can make good choices.

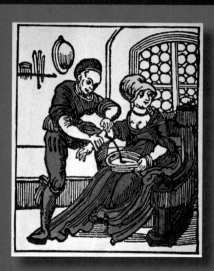

Health Science

Long ago, people believed illness was punishment from the gods. They thought people could only get better by magic or by honoring the spirits. They believed evil needed to escape the body. They drilled a hole in the skull or cut a vein. They thought these things would allow the evil spirits to escape.

◄ The body is made of many different parts. The parts work together in different systems.

The Systems

The human body is like a machine. It has many working parts. Together, these parts can do a lot of work. The parts depend on one another to support the machine. Each part has specific needs and abilities.

Scientists categorize body parts by the work they do. Any community has people who perform different jobs. The body is similar. It has different parts to do different jobs. A community needs all its workers to do their jobs, or there will be trouble. The body needs all its parts to work well, too. If they don't, there will be trouble. The trouble can be illness or injury.

Doctors study many years to learn about medicine. They need to study the different parts of the body. Looking at the different parts helps us understand what they do. Then we can begin to understand the body as a whole.

Doctors are specialists in the systems of the body.

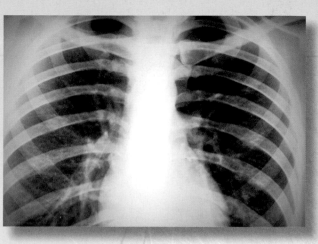

Imaging Techniques

Have you ever thought you broke a bone? Did your doctor take a picture of the bone? Doctors often use machines to look inside the body. They can look inside without surgery. They can take pictures of bones, **organs**, and tissue. They use X-rays, computer tomography (CT Scans), ultrasound, and magnetic resonance imaging (MRI). These and other machines provide instant information to help doctors treat their patients.

Doctors use MRIs and other tools to see the inside of a body.

The Cardiovascular System

The cardiovascular system has many jobs. It keeps blood moving. It keeps the heart beating. It affects body temperatures. This system never rests. The body cannot live without a working heart. The heart supplies blood and oxygen to other organs.

Heart problems can occur when the **arteries** become blocked or narrow. A condition known as coronary artery disease occurs. It can cause chest pain, leading to heart attacks. Smoking, lack of exercise, and poor diets can cause arteries to clog.

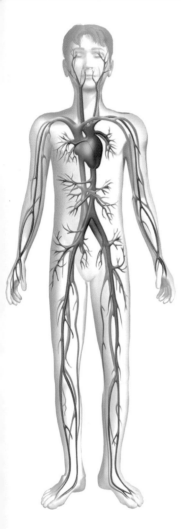

⬆ Your heart is like a pump.

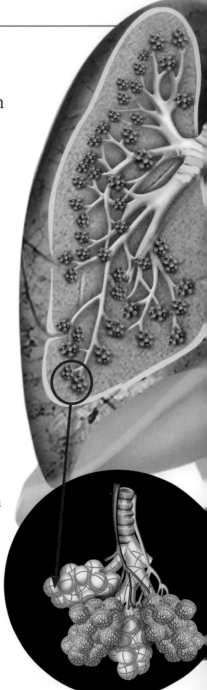

⬆ Alveoli are the tiny air sacs the lungs where oxygen and carbon dioxide are exchang

The heart is an important part of the cardiovascular system.

The Respiratory System

The respiratory system provides the body's oxygen. It draws air into the lungs. Then, oxygen from the air is moved into the blood that is pumped through the lungs by the heart. Carbon dioxide waste from the blood is moved into the air that is then pushed out of the lungs.

The respiratory system is made of several parts. It includes the nose, which draws in air. It also includes the pharynx (throat), larynx (voice box), trachea (windpipe), and the bronchial tubes. The bronchial tubes carry air between the lungs and the outside atmosphere.

A healthy diet helps to create a healthy heart.

A Beating Heart

Have you ever listened to your heartbeat? You can listen through an instrument called a **stethoscope**. Your doctor or a nurse might let you use a stethoscope to hear your own heartbeat. Have you ever felt your heart beat? After heavy exercise, such as fast running or pumping a bicycle up a hill, you might feel a pounding sensation in your chest.

The Digestive System

What happens to the food you eat? You probably already know that it becomes fuel for your body. How does the body use it? The **digestive system** turns food into substances that the body can absorb. Food contains carbohydrates, fats, and proteins. The body uses these nutrients for different purposes.

The digestive process starts in the mouth. The teeth, tongue, and salivary glands grind the food. Then the food enters the body. It goes through the gastrointestinal (GI) tract. The GI tract runs through the body. It is divided into two sections. They are the esophagus and stomach, and the intestines. The gallbladder, liver, and pancreas all help with **digestion**.

The food parts become smaller and smaller as they travel through the body. When the body has taken out as many nutrients as it can, it gets rid of the rest.

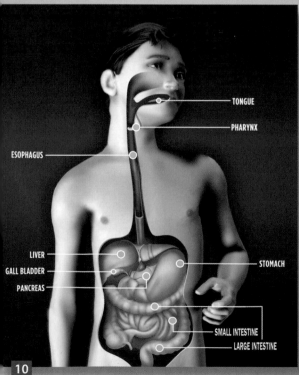

TONGUE

PHARYNX

ESOPHAGUS

LIVER

GALL BLADDER

PANCREAS

STOMACH

SMALL INTESTINE

LARGE INTESTINE

the digestive system

Did You Know?

The cells that line the GI tract work very hard. There is lots of wear and tear on these cells. They are destroyed in just a few days. The body is always replacing these cells.

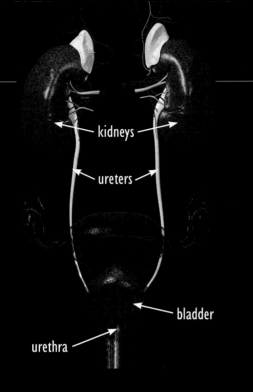

kidneys

ureters

bladder

urethra

The Urinary System

The **urinary system** keeps the body stable. It includes the kidneys and the bladder. The kidneys process blood to remove waste before it builds up and becomes harmful. The bladder stores the urine until it can be released. Urine is about 95 percent water.

Does this sound familiar? The digestive system gets rid of waste, too. We usually think of these as the same thing. They're actually very different. Digestive waste is the remains of food that cannot be used. Urinary waste is byproducts of the body functioning. The body has a different system to get rid of each one.

Location in the Body	Food Processing Time
in the mouth	only a few moments
esophagus and stomach	three to six hours
small intestine	about eight hours
large intestine	12–36 hours

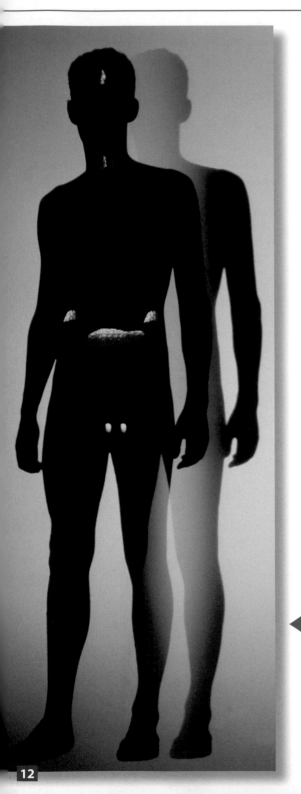

the endocrine system

The Endocrine System

You do not look the same as you did last year. People mature. They go through changes. How does the body know to change? The **endocrine system** controls mood, growth, and development. Hormones are released into the blood. They determine physical changes in the body.

Some hormones are released at specific times. This could be at specific stages of development. Or it might be in reaction to the environment. **Adrenaline** is released in times of stress. Sex hormones are released during puberty, at around 12 years of age. Growth hormones are very active during childhood. They slow down after puberty.

Birth families share genetic traits that include appearance and body chemistry.

The Reproductive System

The endocrine system works closely with the other systems. It works with the **reproductive system**. The reproductive system produces male and female sex cells. It fertilizes eggs that develop in a female's womb. It also nourishes a developing baby.

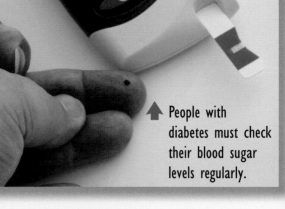

▲ People with diabetes must check their blood sugar levels regularly.

Treating Diabetes

Insulin is one type of hormone. It controls the amount of sugar in your blood. **Diabetes** is a disease that prevents the breakdown of sugar. When the glucose levels in the body rise, the body responds. The body tries to get rid of the glucose through urination. This causes sufferers to be very thirsty.

Diabetes was a fatal disease until 1922. Then, scientists found a treatment. They learned that insulin injections support blood sugar levels. They learned this by working with a special patient. It was a diabetic dog named Marjorie.

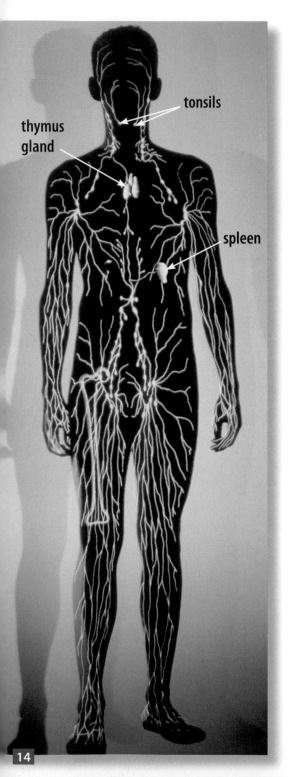

thymus gland

tonsils

spleen

The Immune System

People come in contact with germs and **viruses** every day. Most of the time, they don't get sick. How can we fight off dangers without even thinking about it? The body's **immune system** is its defense. It has lymphocytes, or white blood cells. They act like soldiers, fighting off disease and **infection**. The worse the infection, the more white blood cells are sent out.

The Lymphatic System

The **lymphatic system** includes the lymph nodes, spleen, and tonsils. Lymph nodes fight disease. They are filled with fibers. The fibers destroy **pathogens**, or germs, and cancer cells. The spleen removes germs in the blood. Tonsils block germs from entering the throat. During childhood, the thymus gland helps develop the immune system.

◀ Our body fights off illness every day, using the lymphatic system.

red blood cell

The Mighty Immune System

Lymphocytes, or white blood cells, are created in the bone marrow. They are part of the immune system. They are the body's most powerful defense system for fighting diseases.

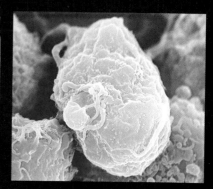

white blood cell

HIV and AIDS

Human Immunodeficiency Virus (HIV) is a virus. It damages cells that help the immune system to work. The body can get **infections.** It can catch other diseases. When this happens, the condition is called Acquired Immunodeficiency Syndrome (AIDS). Drugs have been developed to fight the disease. Like any other disease, prevention is the best defense against AIDS.

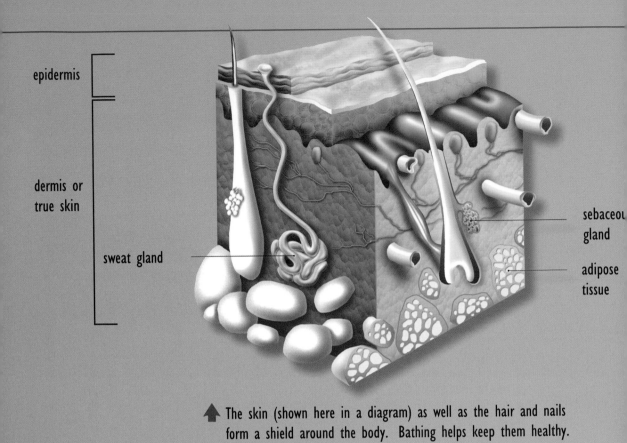

epidermis

dermis or
true skin

sweat gland

sebaceous
gland

adipose
tissue

The skin (shown here in a diagram) as well as the hair and nails
form a shield around the body. Bathing helps keep them healthy.

The Integumentary System

Skin, hair, and nails make up the **integumentary system**.
They protect the body from the outside world.

Skin

The skin is the body's largest organ. It does many things.
It protects the internal organs. It can detect touch. It feels
pain. It also feels hot and cold temperatures. Did you know
the skin also helps control body temperatures?

The skin has two layers. They are the upper layer and the lower layer. The upper layer keeps the body from drying out or becoming "flooded." The lower layer supports hair follicles and sweat glands.

Hair

Almost every part of your body is covered with hair. The hair helps control body temperature. It also protects the head from harmful sunlight. Each person's hair is affected by heredity. Genes play a big part in determining texture, color, and growth.

Nails

The tips of the fingers and toes are very sensitive. The nails are hard plates of protein. They protect and support the fingers and toes. The health of a nail can be a sign of the general health of a person.

Hairy Business

About 100,000 hairs grow from a person's scalp. About 100 hairs are lost each day, and they are replaced by new growth. A hair can grow for several years, and then hit a resting period. Eventually, old hair is pushed out of its follicle by new hair coming in.

Fingerprints

Fingerprints are unique to each person. So, they are good for identifying people. Swirling lines form ridges at the ends of fingers and thumbs. These ridges produce patterns. With oils from the sweat glands, fingers leave "prints" of these patterns on objects that they touch. The prints can be traced back to the person who matches the pattern. This makes them helpful in solving crimes.

The Skeletal System

The **skeletal system** is the framework for the body. It supports the body and gives it shape. It supports muscles tha[t] allow the body to move. All of the bones in a body form the skeleton. The bones are linked by joints

Bones often protect vita[l] organs. For example, the rib cage protects the heart. The skull protects the brain.

The skeletal system also provides substances to aid the immune system.

The Muscular System

The skeleton could not work without the **muscular system**. Muscles perform all body movements. Some muscles attach to bones. Others work on their own. Muscles can get shorter, or **contract**. This creates a pulling force. Most muscles come in pairs. One muscle pulls your body one way. The othe[r] muscle can pull your body the other way. That way you can move back and forth.

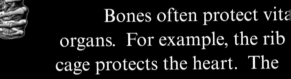

the skeleton

There are three types of muscles. Skeletal muscles are used for activities such as running, lifting, and swimming. These muscles tire easily. The cardiac muscle is found in the wall of the heart. It contracts constantly. It creates a heartbeat. Smooth muscles perform vital functions such as swallowing.

Shivering to Stay Warm

When we get cold, we shiver. These muscle contractions work to make heat for the body.

Bone Up on the Facts

Did you know that your skeleton contains 206 separate bones? The bones differ in size and shape, but they are all active.

If the skeleton were a solid frame that did not bend, we would not be able to move. Our skeleton has more than 400 joints. They connect the bones. These "hinges" in the frame allow us to bend and move.

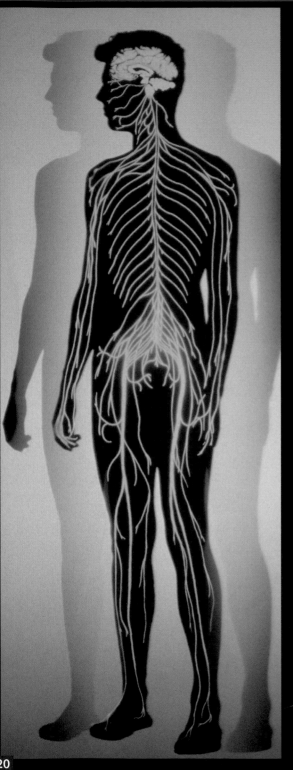

The Nervous System

The brain controls the body, but it does not work alone. It uses the **nervous system**. The nervous system gathers information all day long. It takes information from inside the body. It gathers information from outside the body. Then it reacts. The nervous system sends signals to the muscles. It monitors the organs. It reviews information. Then it makes decisions. It helps to control the entire body.

Neurons carry signals from all over the body. Most neurons are in the brain. The brain is the most complex of all body parts. It controls involuntary activities. These include heartbeats, breathing, and digestion.

◀ the nervous system

◀ neuron

The brain is also responsible for voluntary activities like walking and moving. It even handles conscious activities. These include thought, reasoning, and abstraction.

The brain makes up only two percent of the body, but it controls everything the body does.

Very Nervous

There are more nerve cells in the human brain than there are stars in the Milky Way galaxy.

Instinct and Abstraction

Most animals depend on instincts for survival. Humans are no different. Hunger, fear, and even love come from instincts. Instincts tell us important things about what we need to do to solve problems here and now. Humans can also use abstraction. That means we can think about problems before they happen. We can think about problems afterward, too. We can even stop and think rather than rely on instincts. Sometimes we can think too much!

Emotions

An emotion is an instant response to something. Many things can cause an emotion. An event, a thought, or even a television show can cause an emotion.

Putting Science to Good Use

Good habits start young. You should begin to take care of your body when you are young. Don't wait for health problems to occur. You can prevent many problems. Good habits include eating a healthy diet. They also include getting daily exercise and visiting your doctors.

Adults can help kids reach their fitness goals. Support from friends and family is important. Parents can help teach good eating habits. They can buy and serve foods that are healthy. Friends can get together to exercise. A walk around the block or kicking a soccer ball is always more fun with friends.

However, many activities can be done alone. Dance to your favorite music. Put on an exercise video. Yoga, stretching, and martial arts can be done in your bedroom. Walking up and down stairs is good exercise. Some household chores give a real workout, too!

Sports are a great way to exercise with friends.

Living a Healthier Life

It's easy to start living a healthier life. Think about your lifestyle. Change habits that hold you back from being fit. Keep the habits that lead to good heath.

1. **What should I eat?** A balanced diet is the key to good health. You can't eat too many vegetables. Limit fats and sugars.

2. **Drink lots of water.** Avoid sodas and drinks that are high in sugar.

3. **Keep moving!** Limit your time spent on the computer or watching television. It's easy to forget about the time. Instead of sitting for hours, set a timer. Get up and use your body!

4. **Schedule physical activities.** Sign up for a swim team or exercise class. Staying on a schedule means it's harder to skip sessions. You can also make friends in class and be healthy together.

Safe Sports

An important part of keeping the body healthy and strong is staying active. Playing sports is a great way to stay healthy. They are also fun! Sports provide exercise and friendships. And they teach people to work as a team.

Youth sports should be fun. Safety should also be kept in mind. You can stay safe and healthy if you remember to follow these 10 tips:

1. Play in a safe area.

2. Play under the direction of a trained coach.

3. Play within your limits. Don't try to learn it all in a day!

4. Always wear the right equipment, especially shoes and safety gear.

5. Stretch and warm up before playing.

6. Know the rules of the game.

7. Respect your teammates.

8. Respect the other team.

9. Don't play when you are injured.

10. Cool down slowly after a good workout.

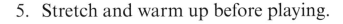 Safety equipment, such as this batter's helmet, keeps sports safe.

Sports for One, Two, or Many

Did you know there are a lot of ways to be active alone? You can play handball or go for a walk. You can take a swim. (Just be sure someone is watching you.) You can practice dribbling a ball. You can golf or jump rope. There are many things you can do.

What if there are two of you? You can have races. You can play catch. You can practice pitching and hitting a baseball. You can go for a bike ride together. Don't forget your helmets!

Sometimes you have a whole group of friends with you. What can you do then? Your options are endless. You can play any sport. Basketball, baseball, and soccer are great fun. But there are plenty more fun things to do! How many can you think of?

Healthcare Professionals

Healthy bodies also sometimes need a doctor's care. Doctors help us be healthy. They provide care when we are sick. They also provide **preventive medicine**. That allows us to avoid diseases. With regular checkups, we can help our doctors help us.

Doctors are ready when you need help. Some doctors practice general medicine. Other doctors treat different illnesses. They work with different parts of the body. They are called specialists. There are doctors who treat children. Other doctors treat the elderly. Some doctors treat the ear, nose, and throat. Others work with the heart.

There are other kinds of healthcare professionals. Nurses help doctors. They can specialize in one type of medicine, too. Dentists take care of our teeth and gums. Psychologists take care of our mental health. Physical therapists help people with physical disabilities.

It's easy to take good health for granted. It takes good decisions and medical experts to keep your body strong.

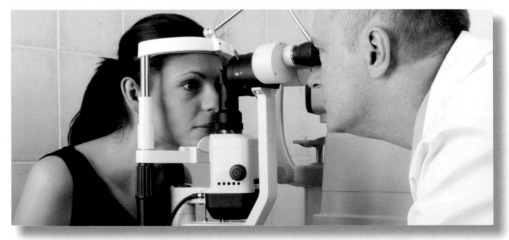

▲ Everyone should have a yearly eye exam.

Physical therapists help people recover from injuries and surgeries. They work with people with physical challenges, and they train athletes.

Consider a Career in Medicine

Do you like helping people? You should consider a career in medicine. You can study to become a doctor. You can also consider other medical fields. Depending on your interests, many careers are available to you. Be sure to keep your grades up. Study hard. Take a lot of science classes.

Some Health Care Professions:

- physician
- nurse
- psychologist
- dentist
- dental assistant
- administrator

- medical assistant
- radiology technician
- research assistant
- massage therapist
- physical therapist
- medical technologist

Lab: The Nose Knows

You will test several people to see if their abilities to smell are equal. Be sure there are no distractions. Ask yourself, is the sense of smell more developed in some people? Or are people who seem to have good noses just more focused?

Materials

- five or more volunteers
  (more volunteers give your experiment better results)
- blindfolds for the volunteers
- three or four fragrant items
  (such as perfume, scented soap, hot popcorn, flowers, warm brownies, garlic, a sliced orange)
- stopwatch or timer
- chart
- pen or pencil

Procedure

1 Find a room in which to conduct your experiment. Make this room as quiet as possible. Turn off radios, televisions, and other noisemakers. Close windows. Turn off anything that affects the airflow in the room (air conditioners, furnaces, etc.).

2 Blindfold your volunteers. Then lead them into the room, two at a time. Place them each about 10 feet from the doorway. Set them in a comfortable position. Tell them to keep quiet and relax.

3 Tell the volunteers to quietly raise their hands whenever they smell a new item. Tell them to think about what the smell may be.

4 Have your charting materials ready. If possible have an assistant record your results.

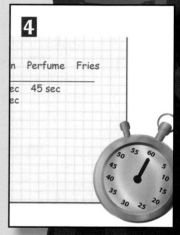

5 Bring the first item into the room and place it just inside the doorway. Spray the bottle if necessary.

6 Record the amount of time that passes before each hand is raised, in seconds. Wait until both volunteers have raised their hands. Ask them to identify the smell. Record their answers.

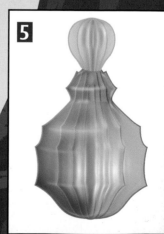

7 Repeat steps 5 and 6, using different items. Vary the time between smells. Try to "trick" them to be sure they are accurately reporting smells.

8 Repeat the test with additional volunteers. Record the results.

Glossary

adrenaline—a hormone produced by the body in times of fear, anger, stress, or excitement, that makes the heart beat faster

artery—blood vessel that runs from the heart to body tissues

contract—shorten or tense up, as with a muscle

diabetes—a disease in which the body cannot control the level of sugar in the blood

digestion—act of breaking down food into simpler substances that can be absorbed into the bloodstream

digestive system—the organs in the body that digest food

endocrine system—bodily system that consists of the endocrine glands, which function to regulate the body's activities

genes—a part of the DNA in a cell that contains information in a special pattern received by each human, animal, or plant from its parents, and that controls its physical development, behaviors, etc.

immune system—the various cells and tissues in the body that make it able to protect itself against infection

infection—establishment of disease in a body

integumentary system—bodily system consisting of the skin and its associated structures, such as the hair and nails

lymphatic system—the interconnected system of spaces and vessels between tissues and organs by which lymph circulates throughout the body

lymphocyte—a white blood cell that boosts the immune system

marrow—fatty tissue that is found in cavities within the bones

muscular system—the bodily system that is composed of skeletal, smooth, and cardiac muscle tissue and functions in movement of the body

nervous system—the system of cells, tissues, and organs that regulates the body's responses to stimuli

neuron—a nerve cell that sends signals to the brain

organ—a body part that has a specific role or job

pathogens—microorganisms such as a virus or fungus that cause disease

preventive medicine—the branch of study and practice that aims at the prevention of disease and the promotion of health

reproductive system—organs and tissues involved in the production and maturation of gametes and in their union and development as offspring

skeletal system—the hard structure (bones and cartilages) that protects the body and internal organs

stethoscope—the instrument used to listen to the heart and other sounds of the body

system—a combination of things or parts that form a complex or solid whole

urinary system—the bodily system that consists of the organs (including the kidneys and bladder) that produce, collect, and eliminate urine

virus—an infectious, nonliving agent that causes diseases

Index

Sally Ride Science

Sally Ride Science™ is an innovative content company dedicated to fueling young people's interests in science. Our publications and programs provide opportunities for students and teachers to explore the captivating world of science—from astrobiology to zoology. We bring science to life and show young people that science is creative, collaborative, fascinating, and fun.

Image Credits